AF797643

Just In Case I Forget...

II

Marya Patrice Sherron

KI PRODUCTIONS

Where every story matters

Copyright © 2024 KI Productions

All rights reserved.

Printed in the United States of America

ISBN: 978-1-961605-34-3

First Edition

Written, Designed, & Edited by Marya Patrice Sherron

No portion of this book may be reproduced, stored in a retrieval system, or transmitted in any form or by any means, electronic, mechanical, photocopy, recording, scanning, or others without permission from the author. If you would like permission to use material from the book, schedule a reading, recording, or class visit, please contact:
maryapatrice@gmail.com.

Belongs to:

PASSWORD TRACKER

Account

Username

Password

Account

Username

Password

Website

Username

Password

Account

Username

Password

Account

Username

Password

Account

Username

Password

Account

Username

Password

Account

Username

Password

Account

Username

Password

Accoint

Username

Password

Account

Username

Password

Account

Username

Password

PASSWORD TRACKER

Account

Username

Password

Account

Username

Password

Website

Username

Password

Account

Username

Password

Account

Username

Password

Account

Username

Password

Account

Username

Password

Account

Username

Password

Account

Username

Password

Accoint

Username

Password

Account

Username

Password

Account

Username

Password

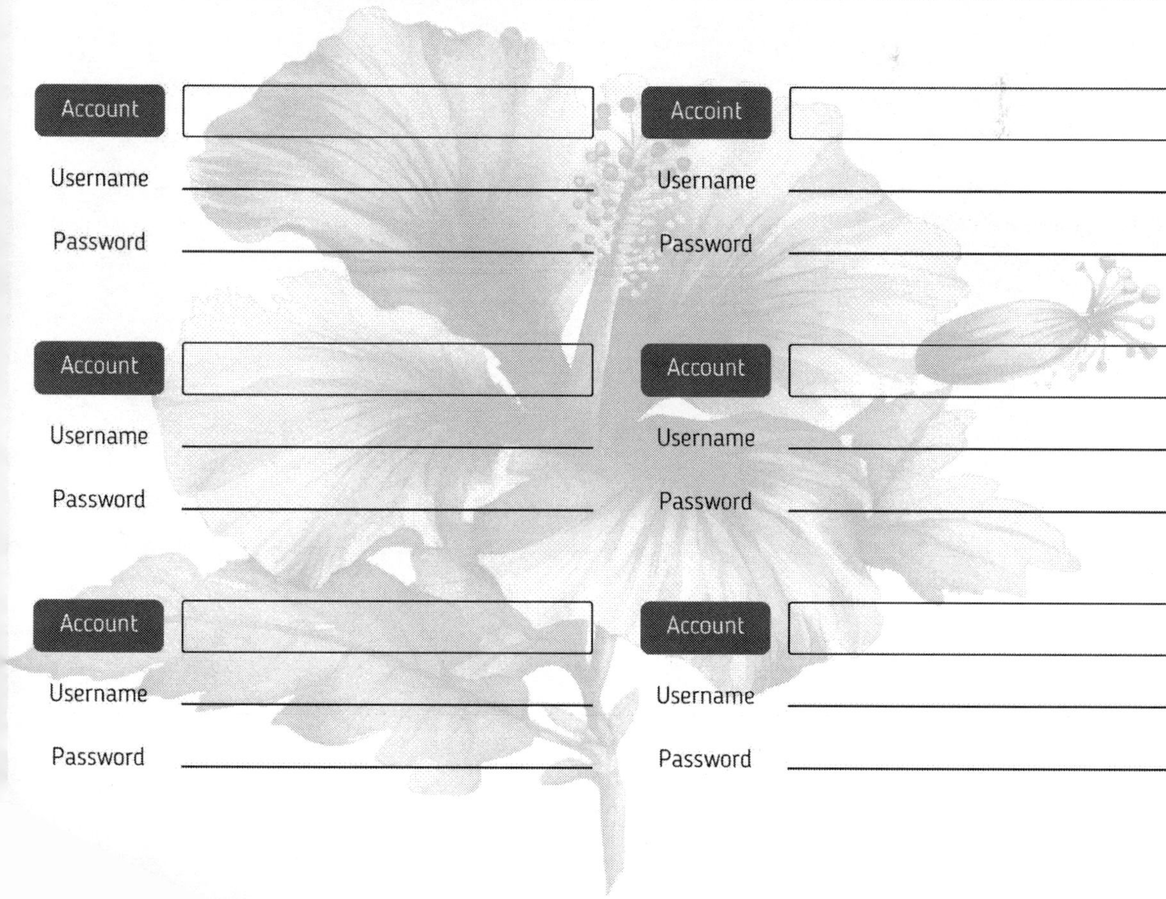

PASSWORD TRACKER

Account

Username

Password

Account

Username

Password

Website

Username

Password

Account

Username

Password

Account

Username

Password

Account

Username

Password

Account

Username

Password

Account

Username

Password

Account

Username

Password

Accoint

Username

Password

Account

Username

Password

Account

Username

Password

PASSWORD TRACKER

Account

Username

Password

Account

Username

Password

Website

Username

Password

Account

Username

Password

Account

Username

Password

Account

Username

Password

Account

Username

Password

Account

Username

Password

Account

Username

Password

Accoint

Username

Password

Account

Username

Password

Account

Username

Password

Notes

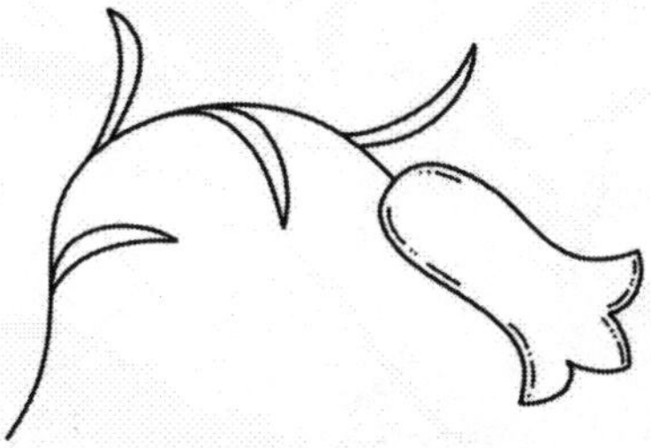

Reminders

PASSWORD TRACKER

Account

Username

Password

Account

Username

Password

Website

Username

Password

Account

Username

Password

Account

Username

Password

Account

Username

Password

Account

Username

Password

Account

Username

Password

Account

Username

Password

Accoint

Username

Password

Account

Username

Password

Account

Username

Password

C

PASSWORD TRACKER

Account

Username

Password

Account

Username

Password

Website

Username

Password

Account

Username

Password

Account

Username

Password

Account

Username

Password

Account

Username

Password

Account

Username

Password

Account

Username

Password

Accoint

Username

Password

Account

Username

Password

Account

Username

Password

PASSWORD TRACKER

Account

Username

Password

Account

Username

Password

Website

Username

Password

Account

Username

Password

Account

Username

Password

Account

Username

Password

Account

Username

Password

Account

Username

Password

Account

Username

Password

Accoint

Username

Password

Account

Username

Password

Account

Username

Password

PASSWORD TRACKER

Account

Username

Password

Account

Username

Password

Website

Username

Password

Account

Username

Password

Account

Username

Password

Account

Username

Password

Account

Username

Password

Account

Username

Password

Account

Username

Password

Accoint

Username

Password

Account

Username

Password

Account

Username

Password

Notes

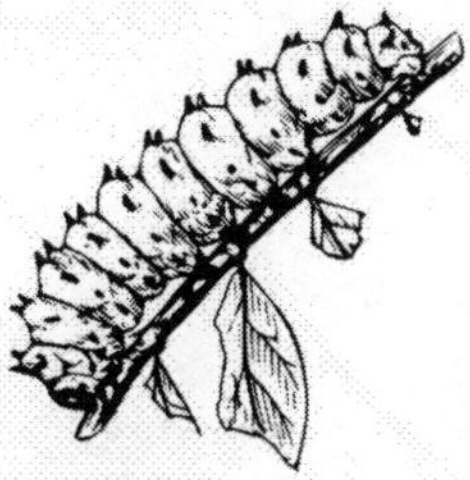

Reminders

PASSWORD TRACKER

Account
Username
Password

Account
Username
Password

Website
Username
Password

Account
Username
Password

Account
Username
Password

Account
Username
Password

Account
Username
Password

Account
Username
Password

Account
Username
Password

Accoint
Username
Password

Account
Username
Password

Account
Username
Password

PASSWORD TRACKER

Account ______

Username ______

Password ______

Account ______

Username ______

Password ______

Website ______

Username ______

Password ______

Account ______

Username ______

Password ______

Account ______

Username ______

Password ______

Account ______

Username ______

Password ______

Account ______

Username ______

Password ______

Account ______

Username ______

Password ______

Account ______

Username ______

Password ______

Accoint ______

Username ______

Password ______

Account ______

Username ______

Password ______

Account ______

Username ______

Password ______

PASSWORD TRACKER

Account

Username

Password

Account

Username

Password

Account

Username

Password

Account

Username

Password

Website

Username

Password

Account

Username

Password

Account

Username

Password

Accoint

Username

Password

Account

Username

Password

Account

Username

Password

Account

Username

Password

Account

Username

Password

PASSWORD TRACKER

Account

Username

Password

Account

Username

Password

Website

Username

Password

Account

Username

Password

Account

Username

Password

Account

Username

Password

Account

Username

Password

Account

Username

Password

Account

Username

Password

Accoint

Username

Password

Account

Username

Password

Account

Username

Password

Notes

Reminders

PASSWORD TRACKER

Account

Username

Password

Account

Username

Password

Website

Username

Password

Account

Username

Password

Account

Username

Password

Account

Username

Password

Account

Username

Password

Account

Username

Password

Account

Username

Password

Accoint

Username

Password

Account

Username

Password

Account

Username

Password

PASSWORD TRACKER

Account ____________________
Username ____________________
Password ____________________

Account ____________________
Username ____________________
Password ____________________

Website ____________________
Username ____________________
Password ____________________

Account ____________________
Username ____________________
Password ____________________

Account ____________________
Username ____________________
Password ____________________

Account ____________________
Username ____________________
Password ____________________

Account ____________________
Username ____________________
Password ____________________

Account ____________________
Username ____________________
Password ____________________

Account ____________________
Username ____________________
Password ____________________

Accoint ____________________
Username ____________________
Password ____________________

Account ____________________
Username ____________________
Password ____________________

Account ____________________
Username ____________________
Password ____________________

PASSWORD TRACKER

Account

Username

Password

Account

Username

Password

Website

Username

Password

Account

Username

Password

Account

Username

Password

Account

Username

Password

Account

Username

Password

Account

Username

Password

Account

Username

Password

Accoint

Username

Password

Account

Username

Password

Account

Username

Password

PASSWORD TRACKER

Account

Username

Password

Account

Username

Password

Website

Username

Password

Account

Username

Password

Account

Username

Password

Account

Username

Password

Account

Username

Password

Account

Username

Password

Account

Username

Password

Accoint

Username

Password

Account

Username

Password

Account

Username

Password

Notes

Reminders

PASSWORD TRACKER

Account

Username

Password

Account

Username

Password

Website

Username

Password

Account

Username

Password

Account

Username

Password

Account

Username

Password

Account

Username

Password

Account

Username

Password

Account

Username

Password

Accoint

Username

Password

Account

Username

Password

Account

Username

Password

H

PASSWORD TRACKER

Account

Username

Password

Account

Username

Password

Website

Username

Password

Account

Username

Password

Account

Username

Password

Account

Username

Password

Account

Username

Password

Account

Username

Password

Account

Username

Password

Accoint

Username

Password

Account

Username

Password

Account

Username

Password

PASSWORD TRACKER

Account

Username

Password

Account

Username

Password

Website

Username

Password

Account

Username

Password

Account

Username

Password

Account

Username

Password

Account

Username

Password

Account

Username

Password

Account

Username

Password

Accoint

Username

Password

Account

Username

Password

Account

Username

Password

PASSWORD TRACKER

Account

Username

Password

Account

Username

Password

Account

Username

Password

Account

Username

Password

Website

Username

Password

Account

Username

Password

Account

Username

Password

Accoint

Username

Password

Account

Username

Password

Account

Username

Password

Account

Username

Password

Account

Username

Password

Notes

Reminders

PASSWORD TRACKER

Account

Username

Password

Account

Username

Password

Website

Username

Password

Account

Username

Password

Account

Username

Password

Account

Username

Password

Account

Username

Password

Account

Username

Password

Account

Username

Password

Accoint

Username

Password

Account

Username

Password

Account

Username

Password

PASSWORD TRACKER

Account

Username

Password

Account

Username

Password

Account

Username

Password

Account

Username

Password

Website

Username

Password

Account

Username

Password

Account

Username

Password

Accoint

Username

Password

Account

Username

Password

Account

Username

Password

Account

Username

Password

Account

Username

Password

PASSWORD TRACKER

Account
Username
Password

Account
Username
Password

Account
Username
Password

Account
Username
Password

Website
Username
Password

Account
Username
Password

Account
Username
Password

Accoint
Username
Password

Account
Username
Password

Account
Username
Password

Account
Username
Password

Account
Username
Password

PASSWORD TRACKER

Account

Username

Password

Account

Username

Password

Website

Username

Password

Account

Username

Password

Account

Username

Password

Account

Username

Password

Account

Username

Password

Account

Username

Password

Account

Username

Password

Accoint

Username

Password

Account

Username

Password

Account

Username

Password

Notes

Reminders

PASSWORD TRACKER

Account

Username

Password

Account

Username

Password

Website

Username

Password

Account

Username

Password

Account

Username

Password

Account

Username

Password

Account

Username

Password

Account

Username

Password

Account

Username

Password

Accoint

Username

Password

Account

Username

Password

Account

Username

Password

PASSWORD TRACKER

Account

Username

Password

Account

Username

Password

Website

Username

Password

Account

Username

Password

Account

Username

Password

Account

Username

Password

Account

Username

Password

Account

Username

Password

Account

Username

Password

Accoint

Username

Password

Account

Username

Password

Account

Username

Password

PASSWORD TRACKER

Account

Username

Password

Account

Username

Password

Website

Username

Password

Account

Username

Password

Account

Username

Password

Account

Username

Password

Account

Username

Password

Account

Username

Password

Account

Username

Password

Accoint

Username

Password

Account

Username

Password

Account

Username

Password

PASSWORD TRACKER

Account

Username

Password

Account

Username

Password

Website

Username

Password

Account

Username

Password

Account

Username

Password

Account

Username

Password

Account

Username

Password

Account

Username

Password

Account

Username

Password

Accoint

Username

Password

Account

Username

Password

Account

Username

Password

Notes

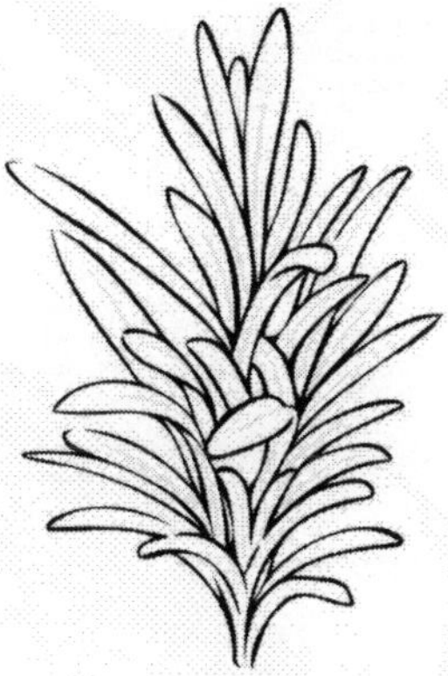

Reminders

PASSWORD TRACKER

Account

Username

Password

Account

Username

Password

Website

Username

Password

Account

Username

Password

Account

Username

Password

Account

Username

Password

Account

Username

Password

Account

Username

Password

Account

Username

Password

Accoint

Username

Password

Account

Username

Password

Account

Username

Password

PASSWORD TRACKER

Account ______________________

Username ______________________

Password ______________________

Account ______________________

Username ______________________

Password ______________________

Website ______________________

Username ______________________

Password ______________________

Account ______________________

Username ______________________

Password ______________________

Account ______________________

Username ______________________

Password ______________________

Account ______________________

Username ______________________

Password ______________________

Account ______________________

Username ______________________

Password ______________________

Account ______________________

Username ______________________

Password ______________________

Account ______________________

Username ______________________

Password ______________________

Accoint ______________________

Username ______________________

Password ______________________

Account ______________________

Username ______________________

Password ______________________

Account ______________________

Username ______________________

Password ______________________

PASSWORD TRACKER

Account

Username

Password

Account

Username

Password

Website

Username

Password

Account

Username

Password

Account

Username

Password

Account

Username

Password

Account

Username

Password

Account

Username

Password

Account

Username

Password

Accoint

Username

Password

Account

Username

Password

Account

Username

Password

PASSWORD TRACKER

Account ______

Username ______

Password ______

Account ______

Username ______

Password ______

Website ______

Username ______

Password ______

Account ______

Username ______

Password ______

Account ______

Username ______

Password ______

Account ______

Username ______

Password ______

Account ______

Username ______

Password ______

Account ______

Username ______

Password ______

Account ______

Username ______

Password ______

Accoint ______

Username ______

Password ______

Account ______

Username ______

Password ______

Account ______

Username ______

Password ______

Notes

Reminders

PASSWORD TRACKER

Account

Username

Password

Account

Username

Password

Website

Username

Password

Account

Username

Password

Account

Username

Password

Account

Username

Password

Account

Username

Password

Account

Username

Password

Account

Username

Password

Accoint

Username

Password

Account

Username

Password

Account

Username

Password

PASSWORD TRACKER

Account

Username

Password

Account

Username

Password

Website

Username

Password

Account

Username

Password

Account

Username

Password

Account

Username

Password

Account

Username

Password

Account

Username

Password

Account

Username

Password

Accoint

Username

Password

Account

Username

Password

Account

Username

Password

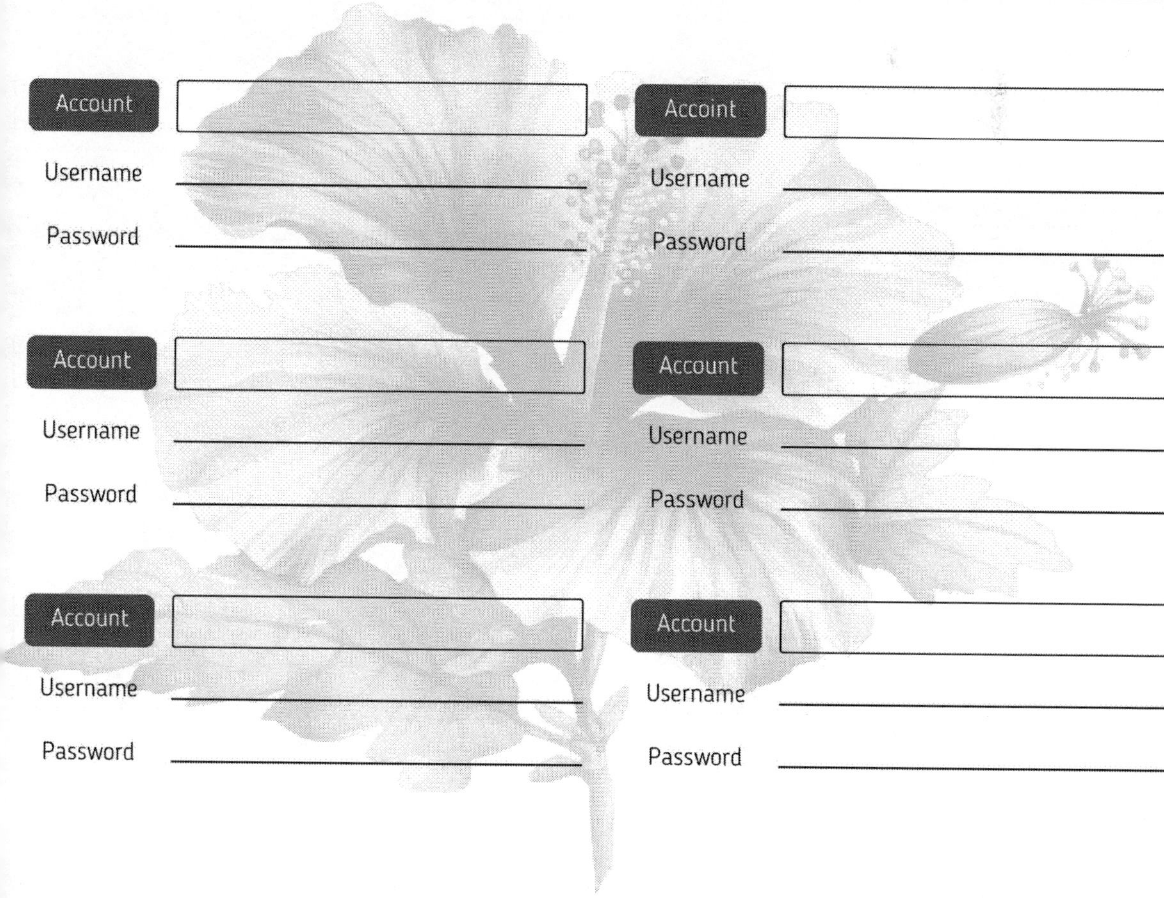

PASSWORD TRACKER

Account

Username

Password

Account

Username

Password

Website

Username

Password

Account

Username

Password

Account

Username

Password

Account

Username

Password

Account

Username

Password

Account

Username

Password

Account

Username

Password

Accoint

Username

Password

Account

Username

Password

Account

Username

Password

Q

PASSWORD TRACKER

Account

Username

Password

Account

Username

Password

Website

Username

Password

Account

Username

Password

Account

Username

Password

Account

Username

Password

Account

Username

Password

Account

Username

Password

Account

Username

Password

Accoint

Username

Password

Account

Username

Password

Account

Username

Password

Notes

Reminders

PASSWORD TRACKER

Account

Username

Password

Account

Username

Password

Account

Username

Password

Account

Username

Password

Website

Username

Password

Account

Username

Password

Account

Username

Password

Accoint

Username

Password

Account

Username

Password

Account

Username

Password

Account

Username

Password

Account

Username

Password

R

PASSWORD TRACKER

Account ______

Username ______

Password ______

Account ______

Username ______

Password ______

Account ______

Username ______

Password ______

Account ______

Username ______

Password ______

Website ______

Username ______

Password ______

Account ______

Username ______

Password ______

Account ______

Username ______

Password ______

Accoint ______

Username ______

Password ______

Account ______

Username ______

Password ______

Account ______

Username ______

Password ______

Account ______

Username ______

Password ______

Account ______

Username ______

Password ______

PASSWORD TRACKER

Account
Username
Password

Account
Username
Password

Website
Username
Password

Account
Username
Password

Account
Username
Password

Account
Username
Password

Account
Username
Password

Account
Username
Password

Account
Username
Password

Accoint
Username
Password

Account
Username
Password

Account
Username
Password

PASSWORD TRACKER

Account
Username
Password

Account
Username
Password

Website
Username
Password

Account
Username
Password

Account
Username
Password

Account
Username
Password

Account
Username
Password

Account
Username
Password

Account
Username
Password

Accoint
Username
Password

Account
Username
Password

Account
Username
Password

Notes

Reminders

PASSWORD TRACKER

Account ______
Username ______
Password ______

Account ______
Username ______
Password ______

Website ______
Username ______
Password ______

Account ______
Username ______
Password ______

Account ______
Username ______
Password ______

Account ______
Username ______
Password ______

Account ______
Username ______
Password ______

Account ______
Username ______
Password ______

Account ______
Username ______
Password ______

Accoint ______
Username ______
Password ______

Account ______
Username ______
Password ______

Account ______
Username ______
Password ______

PASSWORD TRACKER

Account

Username

Password

Account

Username

Password

Website

Username

Password

Account

Username

Password

Account

Username

Password

Account

Username

Password

Account

Username

Password

Account

Username

Password

Account

Username

Password

Accoint

Username

Password

Account

Username

Password

Account

Username

Password

PASSWORD TRACKER

Account

Username

Password

Account

Username

Password

Website

Username

Password

Account

Username

Password

Account

Username

Password

Account

Username

Password

Account

Username

Password

Account

Username

Password

Account

Username

Password

Accoint

Username

Password

Account

Username

Password

Account

Username

Password

PASSWORD TRACKER

Account

Username

Password

Account

Username

Password

Account

Username

Password

Account

Username

Password

Website

Username

Password

Account

Username

Password

Account

Username

Password

Accoint

Username

Password

Account

Username

Password

Account

Username

Password

Account

Username

Password

Account

Username

Password

Notes

Reminders

PASSWORD TRACKER

Account

Username

Password

Account

Username

Password

Website

Username

Password

Account

Username

Password

Account

Username

Password

Account

Username

Password

Account

Username

Password

Account

Username

Password

Account

Username

Password

Accoint

Username

Password

Account

Username

Password

Account

Username

Password

PASSWORD TRACKER

Account

Username

Password

Account

Username

Password

Website

Username

Password

Account

Username

Password

Account

Username

Password

Account

Username

Password

Account

Username

Password

Account

Username

Password

Account

Username

Password

Accoint

Username

Password

Account

Username

Password

Account

Username

Password

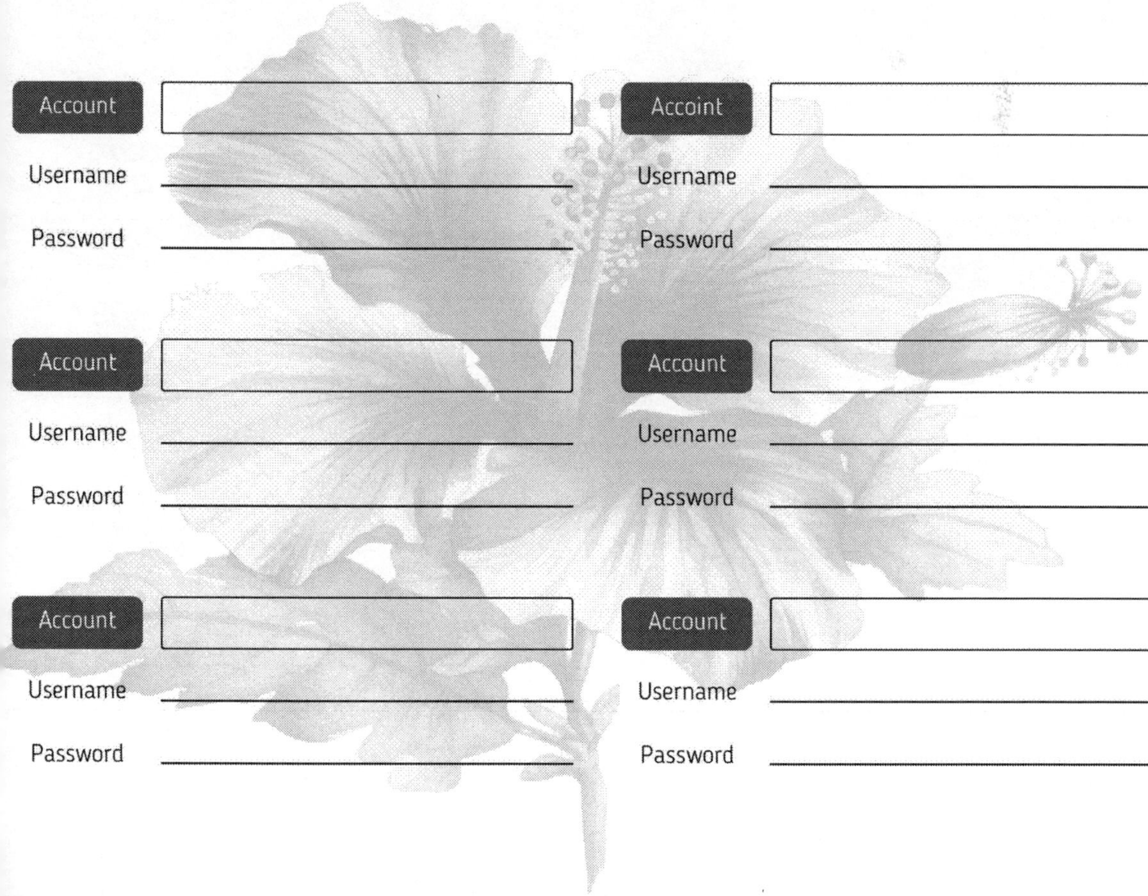

PASSWORD TRACKER

Account

Username

Password

Account

Username

Password

Website

Username

Password

Account

Username

Password

Account

Username

Password

Account

Username

Password

Account

Username

Password

Account

Username

Password

Account

Username

Password

Accoint

Username

Password

Account

Username

Password

Account

Username

Password

W

PASSWORD TRACKER

Account

Username

Password

Account

Username

Password

Website

Username

Password

Account

Username

Password

Account

Username

Password

Account

Username

Password

Account

Username

Password

Account

Username

Password

Account

Username

Password

Accoint

Username

Password

Account

Username

Password

Account

Username

Password

Notes

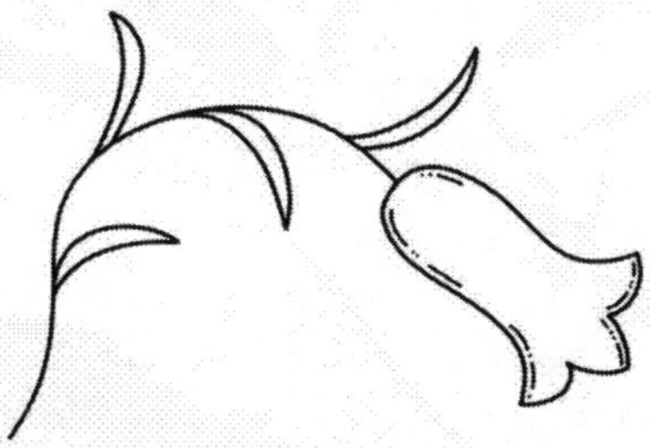

Reminders

PASSWORD TRACKER

Account

Username

Password

Account

Username

Password

Website

Username

Password

Account

Username

Password

Account

Username

Password

Account

Username

Password

Account

Username

Password

Account

Username

Password

Account

Username

Password

Accoint

Username

Password

Account

Username

Password

Account

Username

Password

X

PASSWORD TRACKER

Account
Username
Password

Account
Username
Password

Website
Username
Password

Account
Username
Password

Account
Username
Password

Account
Username
Password

Account
Username
Password

Account
Username
Password

Account
Username
Password

Accoint
Username
Password

Account
Username
Password

Account
Username
Password

PASSWORD TRACKER

Account
Username
Password

Account
Username
Password

Website
Username
Password

Account
Username
Password

Account
Username
Password

Account
Username
Password

Account
Username
Password

Account
Username
Password

Account
Username
Password

Accoint
Username
Password

Account
Username
Password

Account
Username
Password

PASSWORD TRACKER

Account
Username
Password

Account
Username
Password

Website
Username
Password

Account
Username
Password

Account
Username
Password

Account
Username
Password

Account
Username
Password

Account
Username
Password

Account
Username
Password

Accoint
Username
Password

Account
Username
Password

Account
Username
Password

Notes

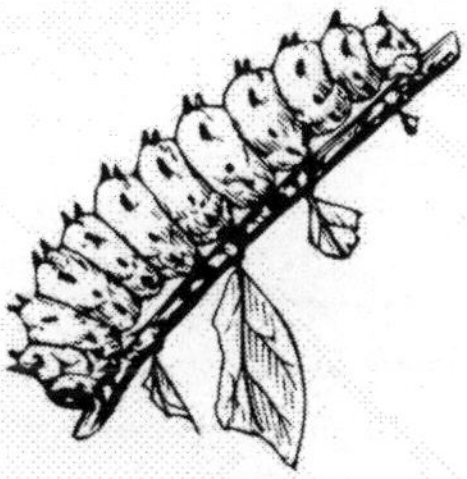

Reminders

PASSWORD TRACKER

Account

Username

Password

Account

Username

Password

Website

Username

Password

Account

Username

Password

Account

Username

Password

Account

Username

Password

Account

Username

Password

Account

Username

Password

Account

Username

Password

Accoint

Username

Password

Account

Username

Password

Account

Username

Password

PASSWORD TRACKER

Account

Username

Password

Account

Username

Password

Account

Username

Password

Account

Username

Password

Website

Username

Password

Account

Username

Password

Account

Username

Password

Accoint

Username

Password

Account

Username

Password

Account

Username

Password

Account

Username

Password

Account

Username

Password

PASSWORD TRACKER

Account ______

Username ______

Password ______

Account ______

Username ______

Password ______

Account ______

Username ______

Password ______

Account ______

Username ______

Password ______

Website ______

Username ______

Password ______

Account ______

Username ______

Password ______

Account ______

Username ______

Password ______

Accoint ______

Username ______

Password ______

Account ______

Username ______

Password ______

Account ______

Username ______

Password ______

Account ______

Username ______

Password ______

Account ______

Username ______

Password ______

Notes

Reminders

PASSWORD TRACKER

Account
Username
Password

Account
Username
Password

Account
Username
Password

Account
Username
Password

Website
Username
Password

Account
Username
Password

Account
Username
Password

Accoint
Username
Password

Account
Username
Password

Account
Username
Password

Account
Username
Password

Account
Username
Password

PASSWORD TRACKER

Account ____________________
Username ____________________
Password ____________________

Account ____________________
Username ____________________
Password ____________________

Account ____________________
Username ____________________
Password ____________________

Account ____________________
Username ____________________
Password ____________________

Website ____________________
Username ____________________
Password ____________________

Account ____________________
Username ____________________
Password ____________________

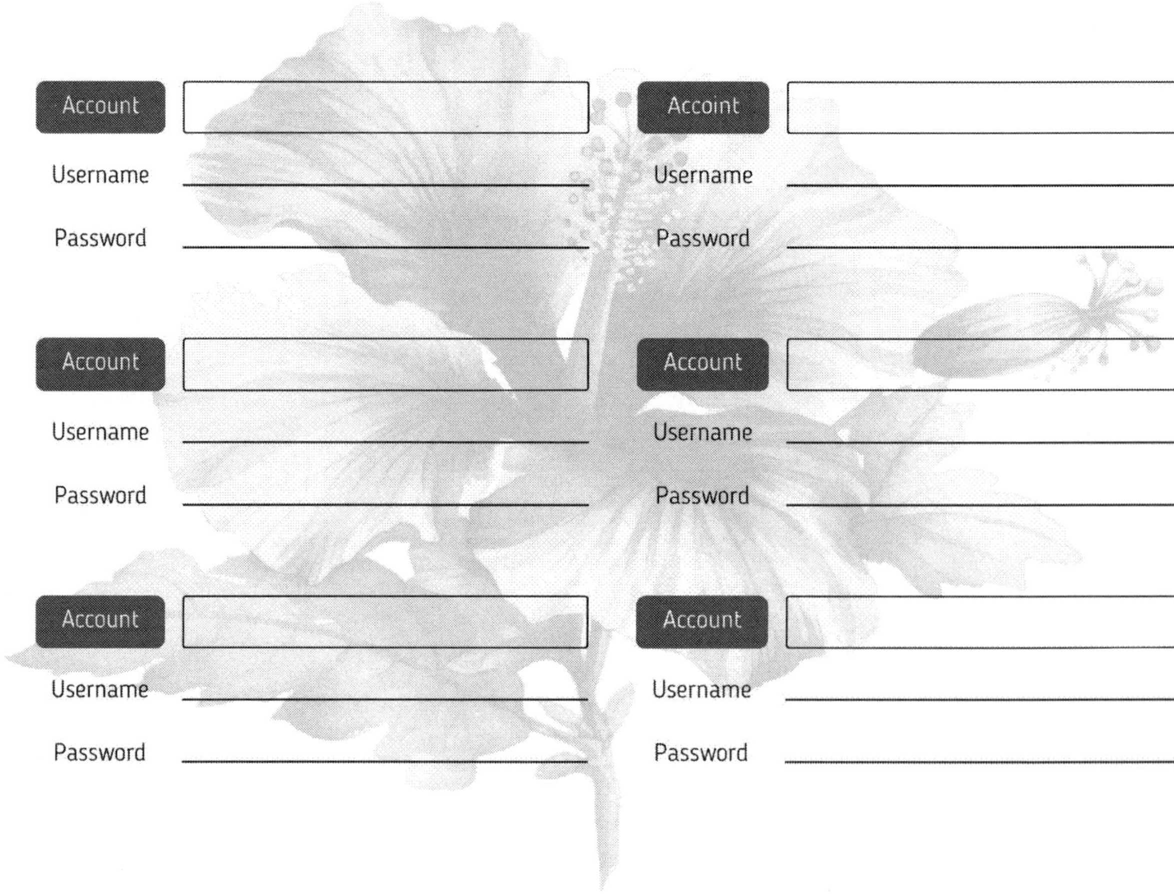

Account ____________________
Username ____________________
Password ____________________

Accoint ____________________
Username ____________________
Password ____________________

Account ____________________
Username ____________________
Password ____________________

Account ____________________
Username ____________________
Password ____________________

Account ____________________
Username ____________________
Password ____________________

Account ____________________
Username ____________________
Password ____________________

PASSWORD TRACKER

Account

Username

Password

Account

Username

Password

Website

Username

Password

Account

Username

Password

Account

Username

Password

Account

Username

Password

Account

Username

Password

Account

Username

Password

Account

Username

Password

Accoint

Username

Password

Account

Username

Password

Account

Username

Password

PASSWORD TRACKER

Account

Username

Password

Account

Username

Password

Website

Username

Password

Account

Username

Password

Account

Username

Password

Account

Username

Password

Account

Username

Password

Account

Username

Password

Account

Username

Password

Accoint

Username

Password

Account

Username

Password

Account

Username

Password

Notes

Reminders

PASSWORD TRACKER

Account

Username

Password

Account

Username

Password

Website

Username

Password

Account

Username

Password

Account

Username

Password

Account

Username

Password

Account

Username

Password

Account

Username

Password

Account

Username

Password

Accoint

Username

Password

Account

Username

Password

Account

Username

Password

PASSWORD TRACKER

Account ____________________
Username ____________________
Password ____________________

Account ____________________
Username ____________________
Password ____________________

Website ____________________
Username ____________________
Password ____________________

Account ____________________
Username ____________________
Password ____________________

Account ____________________
Username ____________________
Password ____________________

Account ____________________
Username ____________________
Password ____________________

Account ____________________
Username ____________________
Password ____________________

Account ____________________
Username ____________________
Password ____________________

Account ____________________
Username ____________________
Password ____________________

Accoint ____________________
Username ____________________
Password ____________________

Account ____________________
Username ____________________
Password ____________________

Account ____________________
Username ____________________
Password ____________________

PASSWORD TRACKER

Account ______________________

Username ______________________

Password ______________________

Account ______________________

Username ______________________

Password ______________________

Account ______________________

Username ______________________

Password ______________________

Account ______________________

Username ______________________

Password ______________________

Website ______________________

Username ______________________

Password ______________________

Account ______________________

Username ______________________

Password ______________________

Account ______________________

Username ______________________

Password ______________________

Accoint ______________________

Username ______________________

Password ______________________

Account ______________________

Username ______________________

Password ______________________

Account ______________________

Username ______________________

Password ______________________

Account ______________________

Username ______________________

Password ______________________

Account ______________________

Username ______________________

Password ______________________

PASSWORD TRACKER

Account

Username

Password

Account

Username

Password

Website

Username

Password

Account

Username

Password

Account

Username

Password

Account

Username

Password

Account

Username

Password

Account

Username

Password

Account

Username

Password

Accoint

Username

Password

Account

Username

Password

Account

Username

Password

Notes

Reminders

PASSWORD TRACKER

Account

Username ______________________

Password ______________________

Account

Username ______________________

Password ______________________

Website

Username ______________________

Password ______________________

Account

Username ______________________

Password ______________________

Account

Username ______________________

Password ______________________

Account

Username ______________________

Password ______________________

Account

Username ______________________

Password ______________________

Account

Username ______________________

Password ______________________

Account

Username ______________________

Password ______________________

Accoint

Username ______________________

Password ______________________

Account

Username ______________________

Password ______________________

Account

Username ______________________

Password ______________________

PASSWORD TRACKER

Account
Username
Password

Account
Username
Password

Account
Username
Password

Account
Username
Password

Website
Username
Password

Account
Username
Password

Account
Username
Password

Accoint
Username
Password

Account
Username
Password

Account
Username
Password

Account
Username
Password

Account
Username
Password

PASSWORD TRACKER

Account

Username

Password

Account

Username

Password

Website

Username

Password

Account

Username

Password

Account

Username

Password

Account

Username

Password

Account

Username

Password

Account

Username

Password

Account

Username

Password

Accoint

Username

Password

Account

Username

Password

Account

Username

Password

PASSWORD TRACKER

Account

Username

Password

Account

Username

Password

Website

Username

Password

Account

Username

Password

Account

Username

Password

Account

Username

Password

Account

Username

Password

Account

Username

Password

Account

Username

Password

Accoint

Username

Password

Account

Username

Password

Account

Username

Password

Notes

Reminders

PASSWORD TRACKER

Account

Username

Password

Account

Username

Password

Website

Username

Password

Account

Username

Password

Account

Username

Password

Account

Username

Password

Account

Username

Password

Account

Username

Password

Account

Username

Password

Accoint

Username

Password

Account

Username

Password

Account

Username

Password

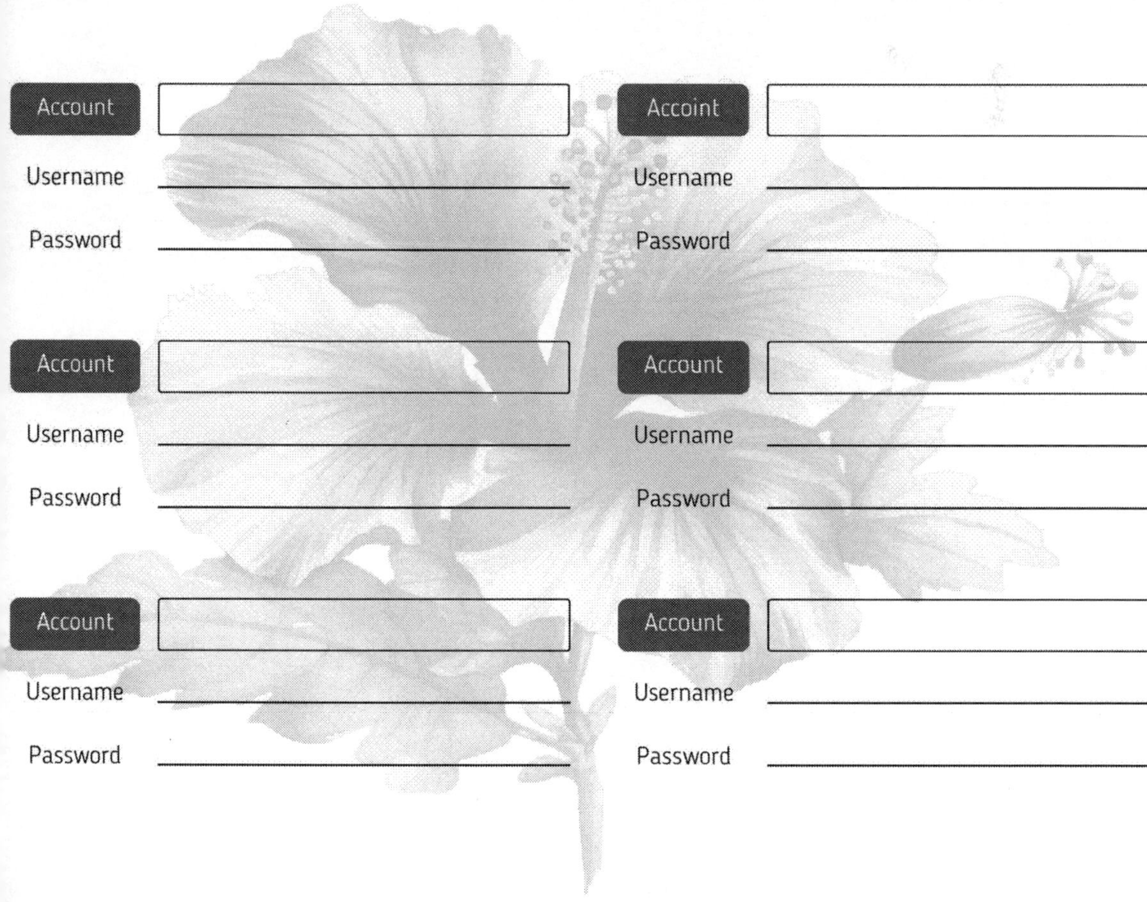

PASSWORD TRACKER

Account ____________

Username ____________

Password ____________

Account ____________

Username ____________

Password ____________

Website ____________

Username ____________

Password ____________

Account ____________

Username ____________

Password ____________

Account ____________

Username ____________

Password ____________

Account ____________

Username ____________

Password ____________

Account ____________

Username ____________

Password ____________

Account ____________

Username ____________

Password ____________

Account ____________

Username ____________

Password ____________

Accoint ____________

Username ____________

Password ____________

Account ____________

Username ____________

Password ____________

Account ____________

Username ____________

Password ____________

PASSWORD TRACKER

Account ________________
Username ________________
Password ________________

Account ________________
Username ________________
Password ________________

Website ________________
Username ________________
Password ________________

Account ________________
Username ________________
Password ________________

Account ________________
Username ________________
Password ________________

Account ________________
Username ________________
Password ________________

Account ________________
Username ________________
Password ________________

Account ________________
Username ________________
Password ________________

Account ________________
Username ________________
Password ________________

Accoint ________________
Username ________________
Password ________________

Account ________________
Username ________________
Password ________________

Account ________________
Username ________________
Password ________________

PASSWORD TRACKER

Account

Username

Password

Account

Username

Password

Website

Username

Password

Account

Username

Password

Account

Username

Password

Account

Username

Password

Account

Username

Password

Account

Username

Password

Account

Username

Password

Accoint

Username

Password

Account

Username

Password

Account

Username

Password

Notes

Reminders

PASSWORD TRACKER

Account

Username

Password

Account

Username

Password

Website

Username

Password

Account

Username

Password

Account

Username

Password

Account

Username

Password

Account

Username

Password

Account

Username

Password

Account

Username

Password

Accoint

Username

Password

Account

Username

Password

Account

Username

Password

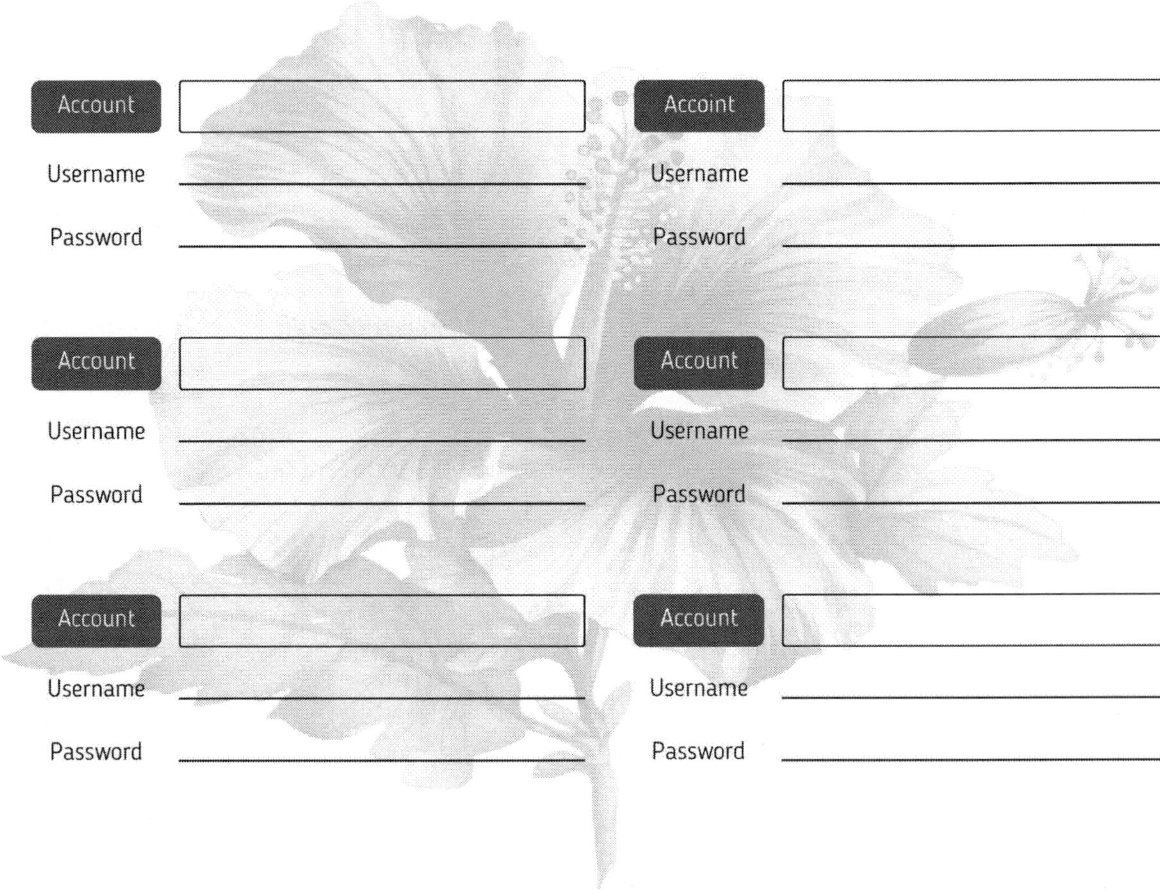

PASSWORD TRACKER

Account

Username

Password

Account

Username

Password

Website

Username

Password

Account

Username

Password

Account

Username

Password

Account

Username

Password

Account

Username

Password

Account

Username

Password

Account

Username

Password

Accoint

Username

Password

Account

Username

Password

Account

Username

Password

PASSWORD TRACKER

Account

Username

Password

Account

Username

Password

Website

Username

Password

Account

Username

Password

Account

Username

Password

Account

Username

Password

Account

Username

Password

Account

Username

Password

Account

Username

Password

Accoint

Username

Password

Account

Username

Password

Account

Username

Password

PASSWORD TRACKER

Account

Username

Password

Account

Username

Password

Website

Username

Password

Account

Username

Password

Account

Username

Password

Account

Username

Password

Account

Username

Password

Account

Username

Password

Account

Username

Password

Accoint

Username

Password

Account

Username

Password

Account

Username

Password

Notes

Reminders

PASSWORD TRACKER

Account

Username

Password

Account

Username

Password

Website

Username

Password

Account

Username

Password

Account

Username

Password

Account

Username

Password

Account

Username

Password

Account

Username

Password

Account

Username

Password

Accoint

Username

Password

Account

Username

Password

Account

Username

Password

PASSWORD TRACKER

Account

Username

Password

Account

Username

Password

Website

Username

Password

Account

Username

Password

Account

Username

Password

Account

Username

Password

Account

Username

Password

Account

Username

Password

Account

Username

Password

Accoint

Username

Password

Account

Username

Password

Account

Username

Password

PASSWORD TRACKER

Account ____________________
Username ____________________
Password ____________________

Account ____________________
Username ____________________
Password ____________________

Website ____________________
Username ____________________
Password ____________________

Account ____________________
Username ____________________
Password ____________________

Account ____________________
Username ____________________
Password ____________________

Account ____________________
Username ____________________
Password ____________________

Account ____________________
Username ____________________
Password ____________________

Account ____________________
Username ____________________
Password ____________________

Account ____________________
Username ____________________
Password ____________________

Accoint ____________________
Username ____________________
Password ____________________

Account ____________________
Username ____________________
Password ____________________

Account ____________________
Username ____________________
Password ____________________

PASSWORD TRACKER

Account

Username

Password

Account

Username

Password

Website

Username

Password

Account

Username

Password

Account

Username

Password

Account

Username

Password

Account

Username

Password

Account

Username

Password

Account

Username

Password

Accoint

Username

Password

Account

Username

Password

Account

Username

Password

Notes

Reminders

PASSWORD TRACKER

Account

Username

Password

Account

Username

Password

Website

Username

Password

Account

Username

Password

Account

Username

Password

Account

Username

Password

Account

Username

Password

Account

Username

Password

Account

Username

Password

Accoint

Username

Password

Account

Username

Password

Account

Username

Password

PASSWORD TRACKER

Account ____________________

Username ____________________

Password ____________________

Account ____________________

Username ____________________

Password ____________________

Website ____________________

Username ____________________

Password ____________________

Account ____________________

Username ____________________

Password ____________________

Account ____________________

Username ____________________

Password ____________________

Account ____________________

Username ____________________

Password ____________________

Account ____________________

Username ____________________

Password ____________________

Account ____________________

Username ____________________

Password ____________________

Account ____________________

Username ____________________

Password ____________________

Accoint ____________________

Username ____________________

Password ____________________

Account ____________________

Username ____________________

Password ____________________

Account ____________________

Username ____________________

Password ____________________

PASSWORD TRACKER

Account

Username

Password

Account

Username

Password

Website

Username

Password

Account

Username

Password

Account

Username

Password

Account

Username

Password

Account

Username

Password

Account

Username

Password

Account

Username

Password

Accoint

Username

Password

Account

Username

Password

Account

Username

Password

PASSWORD TRACKER

Account

Username

Password

Account

Username

Password

Website

Username

Password

Account

Username

Password

Account

Username

Password

Account

Username

Password

Account

Username

Password

Account

Username

Password

Account

Username

Password

Accoint

Username

Password

Account

Username

Password

Account

Username

Password

Notes

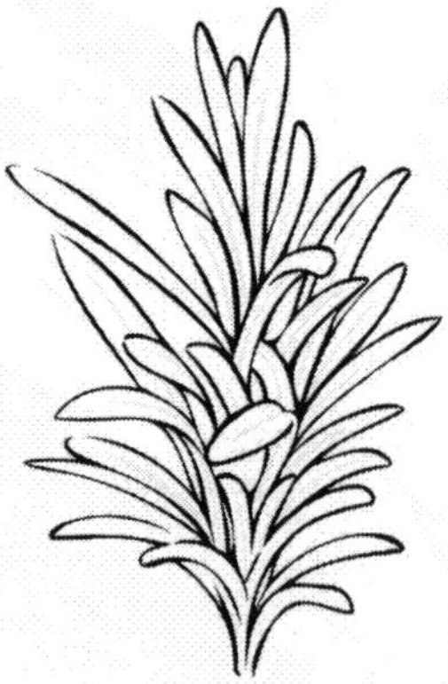

Reminders

PASSWORD TRACKER

Account

Username

Password

Account

Username

Password

Website

Username

Password

Account

Username

Password

Account

Username

Password

Account

Username

Password

Account

Username

Password

Account

Username

Password

Account

Username

Password

Accoint

Username

Password

Account

Username

Password

Account

Username

Password

PASSWORD TRACKER

Account

Username

Password

Account

Username

Password

Website

Username

Password

Account

Username

Password

Account

Username

Password

Account

Username

Password

Account

Username

Password

Account

Username

Password

Account

Username

Password

Accoint

Username

Password

Account

Username

Password

Account

Username

Password

PASSWORD TRACKER

Account

Username

Password

Account

Username

Password

Website

Username

Password

Account

Username

Password

Account

Username

Password

Account

Username

Password

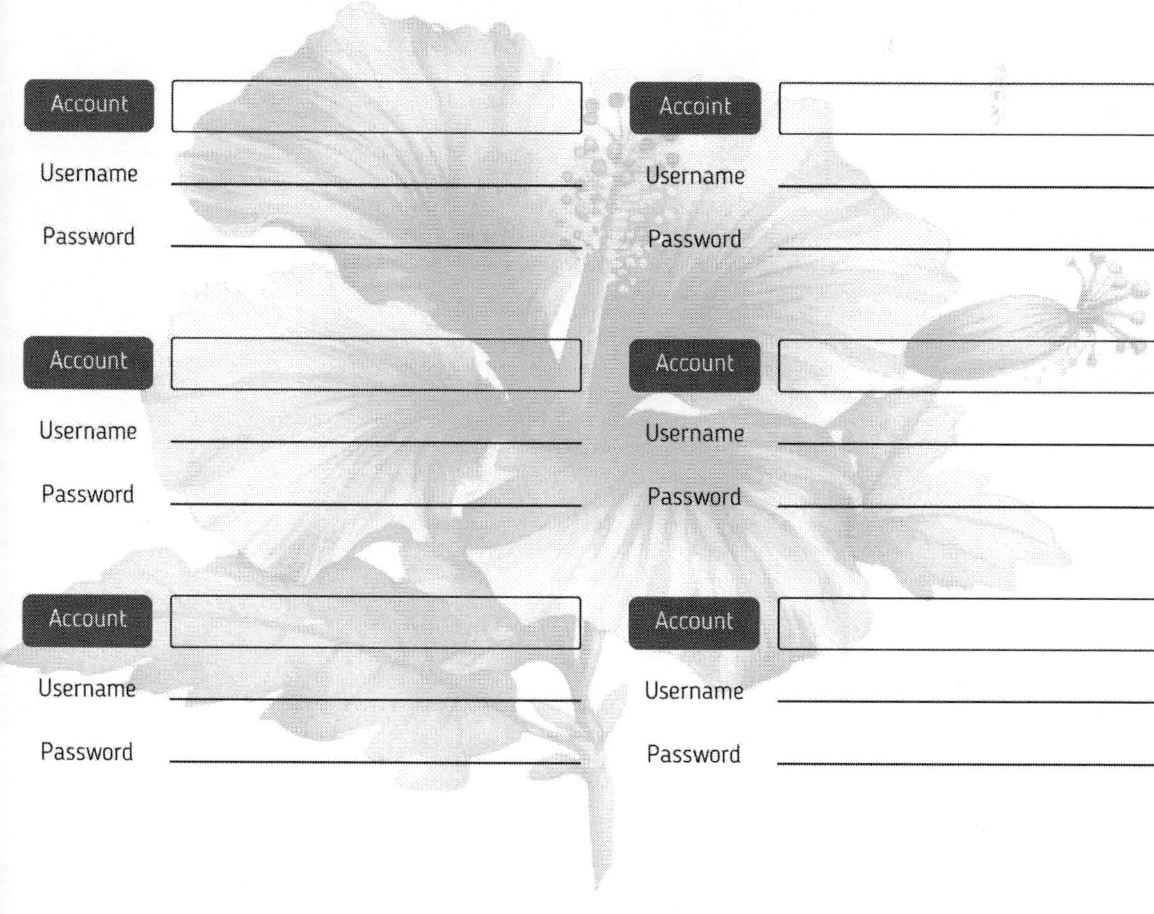

Account

Username

Password

Account

Username

Password

Account

Username

Password

Accoint

Username

Password

Account

Username

Password

Account

Username

Password

PASSWORD TRACKER

Account ____________________
Username ____________________
Password ____________________

Account ____________________
Username ____________________
Password ____________________

Website ____________________
Username ____________________
Password ____________________

Account ____________________
Username ____________________
Password ____________________

Account ____________________
Username ____________________
Password ____________________

Account ____________________
Username ____________________
Password ____________________

Account ____________________
Username ____________________
Password ____________________

Account ____________________
Username ____________________
Password ____________________

Account ____________________
Username ____________________
Password ____________________

Accoint ____________________
Username ____________________
Password ____________________

Account ____________________
Username ____________________
Password ____________________

Account ____________________
Username ____________________
Password ____________________

Notes

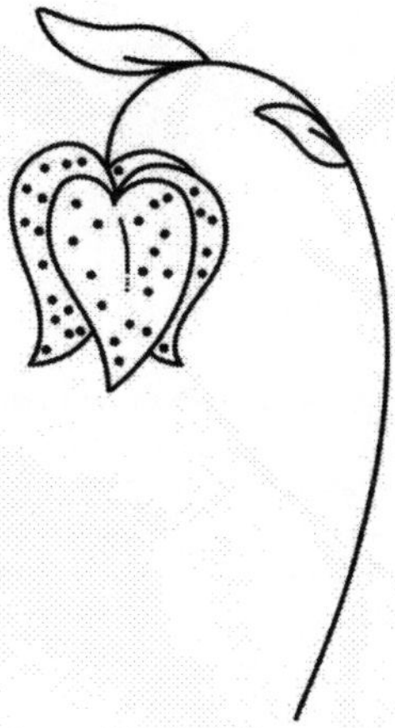

Reminders

PASSWORD TRACKER

Account ______

Username ______

Password ______

Account ______

Username ______

Password ______

Website ______

Username ______

Password ______

Account ______

Username ______

Password ______

Account ______

Username ______

Password ______

Account ______

Username ______

Password ______

Account ______

Username ______

Password ______

Account ______

Username ______

Password ______

Account ______

Username ______

Password ______

Accoint ______

Username ______

Password ______

Account ______

Username ______

Password ______

Account ______

Username ______

Password ______

PASSWORD TRACKER

Account

Username

Password

Account

Username

Password

Website

Username

Password

Account

Username

Password

Account

Username

Password

Account

Username

Password

Account

Username

Password

Account

Username

Password

Account

Username

Password

Accoint

Username

Password

Account

Username

Password

Account

Username

Password

PASSWORD TRACKER

Account ______

Username ______

Password ______

Account ______

Username ______

Password ______

Account ______

Username ______

Password ______

Account ______

Username ______

Password ______

Website ______

Username ______

Password ______

Account ______

Username ______

Password ______

Account ______

Username ______

Password ______

Accoint ______

Username ______

Password ______

Account ______

Username ______

Password ______

Account ______

Username ______

Password ______

Account ______

Username ______

Password ______

Account ______

Username ______

Password ______

PASSWORD TRACKER

Account ____________________
Username ____________________
Password ____________________

Account ____________________
Username ____________________
Password ____________________

Website ____________________
Username ____________________
Password ____________________

Account ____________________
Username ____________________
Password ____________________

Account ____________________
Username ____________________
Password ____________________

Account ____________________
Username ____________________
Password ____________________

Account ____________________
Username ____________________
Password ____________________

Account ____________________
Username ____________________
Password ____________________

Account ____________________
Username ____________________
Password ____________________

Accoint ____________________
Username ____________________
Password ____________________

Account ____________________
Username ____________________
Password ____________________

Account ____________________
Username ____________________
Password ____________________

Month

SUN	MON	TUE	WED	THU	FRI	SAT

Month

SUN	MON	TUE	WED	THU	FRI	SAT

Month

SUN	MON	TUE	WED	THU	FRI	SAT

Month

SUN	MON	TUE	WED	THU	FRI	SAT

Month

SUN	MON	TUE	WED	THU	FRI	SAT

Month

SUN	MON	TUE	WED	THU	FRI	SAT

Month

SUN	MON	TUE	WED	THU	FRI	SAT

Month

SUN	MON	TUE	WED	THU	FRI	SAT

Month

SUN	MON	TUE	WED	THU	FRI	SAT

Month

SUN	MON	TUE	WED	THU	FRI	SAT

Month

SUN	MON	TUE	WED	THU	FRI	SAT

Month

SUN	MON	TUE	WED	THU	FRI	SAT

More Titles by Marya

SELF-HELP & GROWTH

Into the Water: Wading Through Grief

Out of the Water: a Baptism Devotional

Playing in the Dirt & Loving It

Gratitude is the Way

One Year Growth. (peacock-themed) Journal

Autism Love: Journal for Caregivers

Every Crown Has a Story: Tell Your Hair-Story

Be a Pink Dolphin

CHILDREN'S BOOKS

Time to Dance (2-9 years)

Small Big Gifts (1-6 years)

PRAYER JOURNALS

Prayer & Self-Care for Black Women

Prayer & Self-Care for Black Men

Prayer & Self-Care for Women

Prayer & Self-Care for Men

THEMED FULL-COLOR PERSONAL JOURNALS

Butterfly Bliss

Sunny Days.

Magical Moments with Unicorns.

Plant Love in Blue

Plant Lovers Journal

Time to Dream (unicorns)

THEMED BLACK & WHITE PERSONAL JOURNALS

That Black Cat

I Heart Dogs.

I Heart Horses

Black Girl Magic: Mermaids

Crazy Plant Lady Journal

Book Club Journal

Reading Log Journal

Prompts for Creative Writers

VISIT: TIME2DANCE.ORG

@author.maryapatricesherron

Playing
in the Dirt
&
Loving It!
New Release!!!
21
Lessons From My Father's Garden
About Life, Love & Healing
MARYA
PATRICE
SHERRON

Made in the USA
Monee, IL
04 November 2026

67377411R00085